ANSELM GRÜN is a Benedictine monk who has written approximately 300 books that have been translated into 30 different languages. He lives in Germany.

GIULIANO FERRI is an Italian illustrator whose work has been published in Italy, the United States, Japan, and England. His books include *Jonah's Whale* (Eerdmans), *Ant and Grasshopper* (McElderry), *The Story of Daniel in the Lions' Den* (Barefoot Books), and *Small Camel Follows the Star* (Albert Whitman).

© Verlag Herder GmbH, Freiburg im Breisgau 2013
D-79104 Freiburg
www.herder.de
Originally published in German under the title *Jesus*
by Verlag Herder GmbH, 2013
This English language translation © Laura Watkinson

Published in 2014 by Eerdmans Books for Young Readers,
an imprint of Wm. B. Eerdmans Publishing Co.
2140 Oak Industrial Dr. NE
Grand Rapids, Michigan 49505
P.O. Box 163, Cambridge CB3 9PU U.K.

www.eerdmans.com/youngreaders

Manufactured at Tien Wah Press
in Malaysia in September 2013, first printing

19 18 17 16 15 14   9 8 7 6 5 4 3 2 1

ISBN 978-0-8028-5438-4

A catalog record of this book is available from the Library of Congress.

FSC
www.fsc.org
MIX
Paper from
responsible sources
FSC® C012700

JESUS

Written by ANSELM GRÜN

Illustrated by GIULIANO FERRI

Translated by LAURA WATKINSON

Eerdmans Books for Young Readers

Grand Rapids, Michigan • Cambridge, U.K.

OVER two thousand years ago, in the city of Nazareth, there lived a young woman named Mary. She was engaged to a man named Joseph, who was a carpenter. One day, the angel Gabriel came to Mary and said, "Mary, I have good news for you. You are going to have a son, a very special son indeed. People will call him the son of God."

Mary was startled and asked, "How can that be? I'm not even married yet."

But the angel smiled and said, "God makes things possible even when they seem impossible to human beings. He himself will make sure that this happens."

WHAT the angel had said came true, and Mary became pregnant.

Soon after that, the emperor ordered everyone to return to the city of their birth to register for taxes. Mary and Joseph set out on the long journey to Bethlehem.

After traveling for several days, they finally arrived. But when they looked for a place to stay, all of the inns were full. Only one innkeeper took pity on the two of them. He led them to his stable, where his ox and his donkey lived.

And that was where Mary gave birth to her son. She gave him the name Jesus. Mary wrapped Jesus up snugly and laid him in a manger.

WHEN Jesus was twelve, his parents took him to
Jerusalem for the feast of Passover. After the celebrations had
finished, they set off on the journey home. But when Mary and
Joseph looked for Jesus that evening, they could not find him in the
crowd they were traveling with. And so they went back to Jerusalem
to look for him there. After three days, they finally found him at
the temple. He was sitting with the teachers, listening to them and
asking questions. And everyone who heard him was amazed by the
boy's wisdom.

When Jesus saw his parents, he said, "Why were you searching
for me? Didn't you know I would be in my Father's house?"

WHEN Jesus grew up, he left home. He journeyed through the land and told people about God. One day, as Jesus was walking along the shore of the Sea of Galilee, he saw two brothers catching fish with their nets. He said to them, "Follow me! And I will make you fishers of men."

The two brothers put down their nets and went with Jesus.

As he traveled, Jesus met other people who wanted to go with him. Everywhere Jesus and his disciples went, they spread the good news about God.

ONE day, Jesus spoke to a large crowd. In the evening, his disciples said to him, "Send the people away so that they can buy food."

But Jesus answered, "You give them something to eat."

And they replied, "We don't have enough money to buy bread for everyone."

Jesus asked, "How many loaves do you have?"

The disciples counted and replied, "Five loaves of bread and two fish."

Jesus took the five loaves and the two fish and blessed them. He broke the bread and gave the food to his disciples to share among the people. And everyone ate and was satisfied, even though it was a crowd of five thousand.

ONCE, Jesus told a story about a young man who asked his father for a share of his wealth. He wanted to go out into the world and enjoy life. But soon he had spent all of the money and things were going very badly for him. He took a job looking after pigs, but he was still starving. Then he thought of his father and decided to ask for forgiveness.

When the father saw his son, he hugged and kissed him. He was very happy that his son had returned safe and sound, and he held a feast to celebrate.

But when the young man's older brother heard about this, he was very angry. He had worked for his father for many years and never received anything in return. His father told him, "What is mine is yours. But now we must celebrate, because your brother was lost and now he is found."

ONE time, when Jesus was speaking to the people in a village, some of the mothers brought their children to him and asked him to bless the little ones. The disciples were angry. They scolded the parents and told them not to bother Jesus with their children.

But Jesus himself became angry and said to his disciples, "Let the children come to me. The kingdom of God belongs to them. If you do not become like a child, you cannot enter God's kingdom."

Then he embraced each child, placing his hands upon them and blessing them. And God's love wrapped around the children and protected them.

WHILE he traveled, Jesus healed many sick people. One day, a man came to Jesus and said, "My little daughter is ill. Please come and place your hands on her so that she will be healed and live." So Jesus immediately set out with the man for his house. The man's relatives came out to meet them and said to the man, "Your daughter is dead. There is no need for Jesus to come to the house now."

But Jesus said, "Have no fear, and trust in God."

When they reached the house, Jesus took the girl by the hand and said, "My child, get up!" The girl immediately stood up and began to walk around. And everyone was amazed by this miracle.

ONE day, Jesus went to Jericho. A man named Zacchaeus lived in the city. He was the chief tax collector and he was very rich. Most people did not like him because he always wanted too much money from them.

Zacchaeus had heard of Jesus and wanted to see him, but he was so small that he could not see through the crowd. So he climbed up into a sycamore tree. Zacchaeus was hidden among the leaves, but Jesus stopped beneath the tree and called up to him, "Zacchaeus, come down here right now! I would like to come to your home today, as your guest."

Zacchaeus was very happy. He said to Jesus, "Lord, I have done many bad things. But now I want to give half of my money to the poor. And if I have cheated anyone, I will give them back four times as much." And together with Jesus, Zacchaeus celebrated and was full of joy.

JESUS traveled to Jerusalem with his disciples for the Passover feast. He rode into the city on a young donkey. Many people came out to meet him and spread their cloaks on the ground before him. They sang, "Blessed is he who comes in the name of the Lord!"

But not everyone was happy about his arrival. The high priests were angry with Jesus and plotted to kill him.

Even as Jesus feasted at Passover with his disciples, he knew that he would soon die. So he said to them, "Whenever you break bread and drink wine together, think of me."

JUDAS, one of the disciples, had betrayed Jesus to the high priests. He had told them they would find Jesus in the Garden of Gethsemane after the meal. Judas gave Jesus a kiss to show the soldiers which man to arrest.

The next day, the soldiers led Jesus to the Hill of Golgotha, which was outside the city. They crucified him there, between two criminals. As he was hanging on the cross, Jesus prayed for his enemies: "Father, forgive them, for they do not know what they are doing."

Finally, Jesus said, "Father, I commit my spirit into your hands," and he died.

ON the first day of the week, some women went to Jesus'
tomb to anoint his body with spices. But when they got there,
they saw that the stone was rolled away from the tomb. They
went inside, but did not find Jesus there. Then an angel came to
them and said, "Do not fear! Jesus is no longer in the grave. He
has risen!"

Joyfully, the women ran to the disciples to tell them the news.
But the disciples did not believe them.

It was only when Jesus appeared to them that evening as
they were eating that they realized the women had told the
truth: Jesus lives and has triumphed over death!